FRANCIS POULENC

Sonata for Two Clarinets

CHESTER MUSIC

3

SONATA
for Two Clarinets (B♭ and A)

I. Presto

Francis Poulenc
(1918)

CH00219

4

Beaucoup moins vite _ Comme une cadence (♩=80)

II. Andante

III. Vif

Printemps 1918-Boulogne sur Seine

| Flute | Editor: Trevor Wye | | Clarinet | Editor: Thea King |
| Oboe | Editor: James Brown | | Bassoon | Editor: William Waterhouse |

Saxophone   Editor: Paul Harvey

A growing collection of volumes from Chester Music, containing a
wide range of pieces from different periods.

<table>
<tr><td colspan="2">CLARINET SOLOS VOLUME I</td><td colspan="2">CLARINET SOLOS VOLUME II</td></tr>
<tr><td>Bizet</td><td>Entr'acte
from Carmen</td><td>Beethoven</td><td>Allegro (Finale)
from Wind Sextet Op. 71</td></tr>
<tr><td>Labor</td><td>Allegretto
from Quintet for Clarinet,
Strings and Piano</td><td>Crusell</td><td>Minuet
from Quartet in C minor
Op. 4</td></tr>
<tr><td>Lefèvre</td><td>Allegro from Sonata No. 3</td><td>Crusell</td><td>Andante Moderato
from Concerto in Bb Op. 1</td></tr>
<tr><td>Mozart</td><td>Minuet
from Serenade for Wind
Octet K. 375</td><td>Glazounov</td><td>Allegretto
from the ballet
The Seasons</td></tr>
<tr><td>Mozart</td><td>Il Mio Tesoro</td><td>Mendelssohn</td><td>Andante
from Konzertstück in D minor
Op. 114</td></tr>
<tr><td>Schubert</td><td>Trio
from the Minuet of Octet,
Op. 166</td><td>Molter</td><td>Moderato
from Concerto in D</td></tr>
<tr><td>Schubert</td><td>Allegretto
from Symphony No. 3</td><td>Rimsky-
Korsakov</td><td>Andante
from Concerto for Clarinet
and Military Band</td></tr>
<tr><td>Tchaikovsky</td><td>Allegro Con Grazia
from Symphony No. 6</td><td>Weber</td><td>From Introduction, Theme and
Variations</td></tr>
</table>

Also available:
CLARINET DUETS VOLUMES I, II & III
Further details on request

CHESTER MUSIC